Theory Paper Grade 5   2010   A
Model Answers

1   (a) Bar 1: $\frac{3}{8}$ Bar 3: $\frac{2}{4}$ / $\frac{4}{8}$ (4)

(b) five demisemiquavers in the time of four demisemiquavers /   (2)
      five demisemiquavers in the time of two semiquavers /
      five demisemiquavers in the time of one quaver /
      five 32nd notes in the time of four 32nd notes /
      five 32nd notes in the time of two 16th notes /
      five 32nd notes in the time of one eighth note

(c)    (3)

(d) 1 minor 7th   (2)
    2 augmented 4th   (2)
    3 major 3rd   (2)

2   (10)

3   (a) (i)   sad / doleful / sorrowful / mournful   (2)
          with mutes / muted   (2)
          down-bow   (2)
    (ii)   compound   (2)
          duple

(iii)

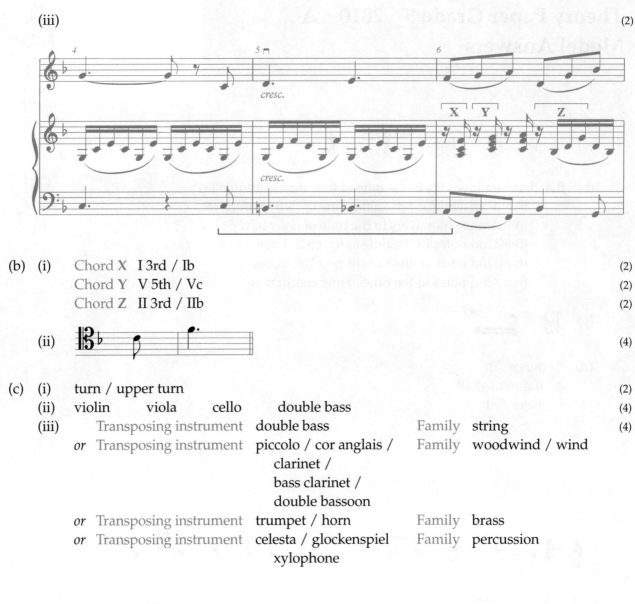

(b) (i) Chord **X** I 3rd / Ib (2)
         Chord **Y** V 5th / Vc (2)
         Chord **Z** II 3rd / IIb (2)

(ii) (4)

(c) (i) turn / upper turn (2)
    (ii) violin   viola   cello   double bass (4)
    (iii)   Transposing instrument double bass   Family string (4)
         or   Transposing instrument piccolo / cor anglais /   Family woodwind / wind
                                         clarinet /
                                         bass clarinet /
                                         double bassoon
         or   Transposing instrument trumpet / horn   Family brass
         or   Transposing instrument celesta / glockenspiel   Family percussion
                                         xylophone

4 (10)

(a)

(b)

5 (10)

Shostakovich

6 *There are many ways of completing this question. Either of the specimen completions below would receive full marks.* (15)

EITHER

(a) violin

OR

(b)

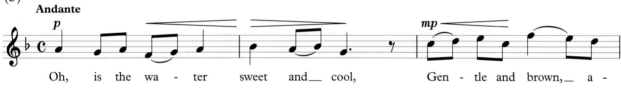

Oh, is the wa - ter sweet and — cool, Gen - tle and brown, — a -

- bove ——— the pool?

7 **EITHER** (10)

(a) Chord A IV / F major   Chord C II / D minor
    Chord B I / C major   Chord D I / C major
                  Chord E V / G major

OR

(b)

5

Theory Paper Grade 5   2010   B
Model Answers

1 (a) (i)   Bar 1: **4/4** / **2/2** / **C** / **¢**   Bar 2: **5/4**   (4)

   (ii)   18   (2)

   (b) (i)   (5)

   (ii)   **A** submediant   **B** mediant   (4)

2 1 minor 10th / compound minor 3rd   (10)
    2 diminished 3rd
    3 augmented 2nd
    4 diminished 7th
    5 perfect 5th

3   (10)

4 (a) (i) moderate speed / moderately   (2)
               graceful / gracefully / with grace   (2)
               repeat from bar 2 / repeat the section / repeat from ‖: / repeat bars 2–9   (2)

        (ii) 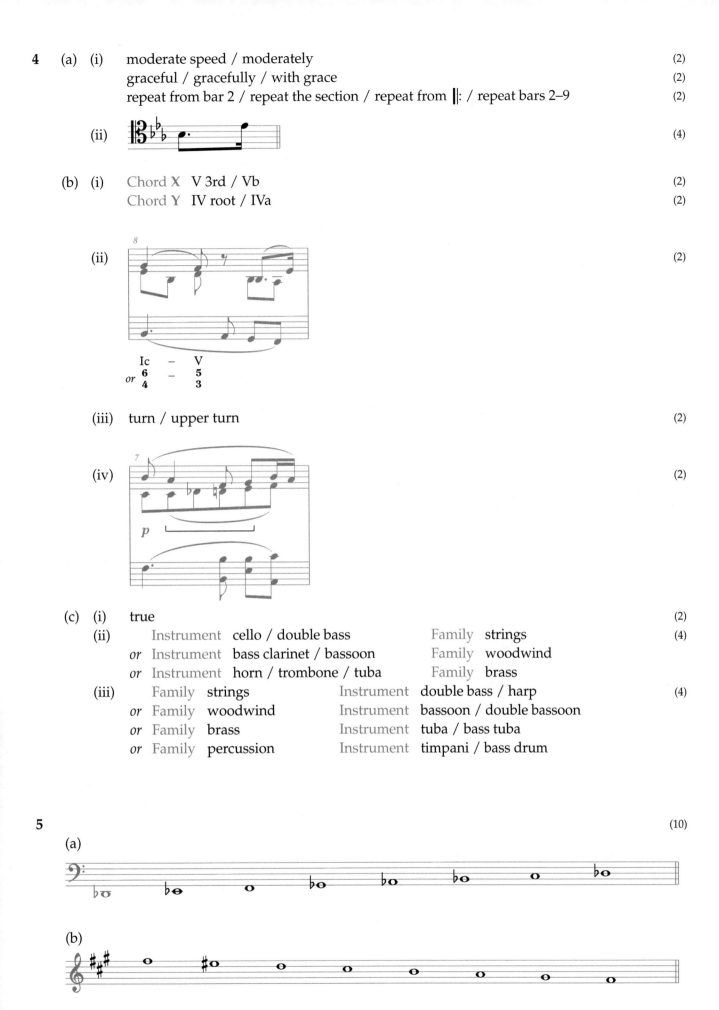   (4)

    (b) (i) Chord **X** V 3rd / Vb   (2)
              Chord **Y** IV root / IVa   (2)

        (ii)   (2)

                Ic   –   V
            or 6   –   5
                 4   3

        (iii) turn / upper turn   (2)

        (iv)   (2)

                p

    (c) (i)   true   (2)
        (ii)   Instrument cello / double bass   Family strings   (4)
            or   Instrument bass clarinet / bassoon   Family woodwind
            or   Instrument horn / trombone / tuba   Family brass
        (iii)   Family strings   Instrument double bass / harp   (4)
            or   Family woodwind   Instrument bassoon / double bassoon
            or   Family brass   Instrument tuba / bass tuba
            or   Family percussion   Instrument timpani / bass drum

5   (10)

    (a)

    (b)

7

6   *There are many ways of completing this question. Either of the specimen completions below would receive full marks.*   (15)

EITHER

(a)   bassoon

OR

(b)

A   wind_____   sways_____   the___   pines,   And   be -

- low_____   Not   a   breath_____   of   wild_____   air.

7   **EITHER**   (10)

(a)   Chord A   II / A minor   Chord D   IV / C major
      Chord B   V / D major   Chord E   I / G major
      Chord C   I / G major

OR

(b)

8

Theory Paper Grade 5   2010   C
Model Answers

1   (a)   (i)    (2)

         (ii)   enough fast / sufficiently fast / quite fast / fairly fast / very fast /   (4)
                extremely fast

         (iii)   (3)

   (b)   (i)   Chord **A**   IV 3rd / IVb   Chord **B**   II 3rd / IIb   (4)

         (ii)    (2)

2   1   diminished 12th / compound diminished 5th   (10)
       2   augmented 4th
       3   minor 7th
       4   major 6th
       5   augmented 2nd

3   (10)

4 **(a)** **(i)** quick and animated / quick and lively / fast and animated / (2)
fast and lively / cheerful and animated / cheerful and lively

forced / forcing / accented (2)

playful / humorous (2)

(ii)  (2)

(iii)  (2)

(b) **(i)**

B	Bar	8	(2)
C	Bar	3	(2)
D	Bar	8	(2)

(ii) (4)

(c) (i) false (2)

false (2)

(ii)   Family **strings**   Instrument **violin** (4)

or Family **brass**   Instrument **trumpet**

or Family **percussion**   Instrument **celesta / glockenspiel / xylophone**

(iii) **timpani / kettledrums / xylophone / glockenspiel / vibraphone / tubular bells /** (2)
marimba / celesta

5 (10)

(a)

(b)

6 *There are many ways of completing this question. Either of the specimen completions below would receive full marks.* (15)

EITHER

(a) oboe

OR

(b)

Now is this song both sung____ and past: My lute! Be still, for____

I have done.

7 EITHER

  (a) Chord A V / A major   Chord C II / E minor

         Chord B I / D major   Chord D I / D major

                                 Chord E V / A major

OR

(b)

Theory Paper Grade 5   2010   S
Model Answers

1 (a) (i)   Bar 2: 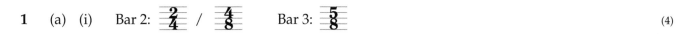 / 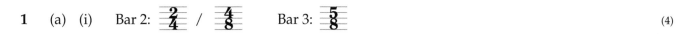   Bar 3: 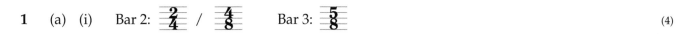   (4)

(ii)   (3)

(b) (i)   1 augmented 4th   (2)
2 minor 9th / compound minor 2nd   (2)
3 minor 6th   (2)

(ii)   to hold the note for an extra three quarters of its original value /   (2)
add on half of the note value plus half of the value of the first dot /

2   (10)

3 (a) (i)   smoothly / without tonguing / slurred   (2)
in a singing style   (2)
freedom of time / free time / robbed time / with some freedom of time   (2)

(ii)   (4)

(b) (i)   A♭ major   (2)
F   (2)
A♭ / A flat   (2)
major 7th   (2)

(ii)   / ... / ... /   (2)

(c) (i)   Instrument cello / double bass   Family strings   (4)

       or Instrument trombone / bass trombone   Family brass

(ii)   false   (2)

      false   (2)

      false   (2)

4   (10)

(a)

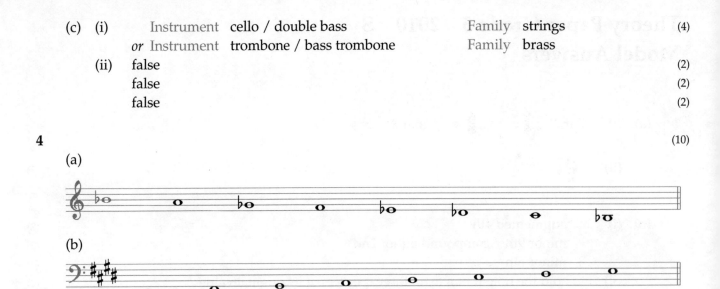

(b)

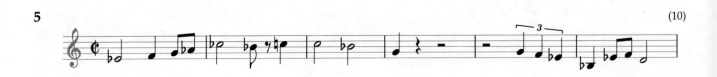

5   (10)

6 *There are many ways of completing this question. Either of the specimen completions below would receive full marks.* (15)

EITHER

(a)   trombone

OR

(b)

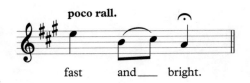

14

7 EITHER

(a) Chord A IV / G major   Chord C II / E minor
    Chord B I / D major   Chord D V / A major
                          Chord E I / D major

OR

(b)

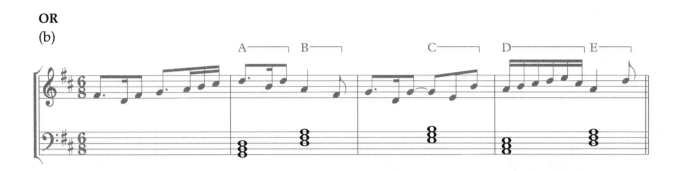

Support material for ABRSM Music Theory exams

Theory of Music Exams
Past Papers
Grades 1 to 8 (separately)

Music Theory in Practice
Grades 1 to 8 (separately)

Music Theory in Practice
Model Answers
Grades 1 to 5 (separately)

The AB Guide to
Music Theory
Parts I and II

First Steps in
Music Theory
Grades 1–5

ABRSM's mission is to motivate musical achievement. We aim to support the development of learners and teachers in music education worldwide and to celebrate their achievements. We do this through authoritative and internationally recognized assessments, publications and professional development support for teachers, and through charitable donations.

ABRSM
24 Portland Place
London W1B 1LU
United Kingdom

www.abrsm.org

Published by ABRSM (Publishing) Ltd,
a wholly owned subsidiary of ABRSM

Printed in England by Halstan & Co. Ltd,
Amersham, Bucks 11/11

ISBN 978-1-84849-298-1